# THE BYZANTINE EMPIRE

## A Society that Shaped the World

**Kelly Rodgers**

## Publishing Credits

Dona Herweck Rice, *Editor-in-Chief*
Lee Aucoin, *Creative Director*
Torrey Maloof, *Editor*
Neri Garcia, *Senior Designer*
Stephanie Reid, *Photo Researcher*
Rachelle Cracchiolo, M.S.Ed., *Publisher*

## Image Credits

## Teacher Created Materials

5301 Oceanus Drive
Huntington Beach, CA 92649-1030
http://www.tcmpub.com

### ISBN 978-1-4333-5001-6
© 2013 Teacher Created Materials, Inc.

# Table of Contents

# A Divided Empire

The Roman Empire was one of the world's first **superpowers**. During its peak, it controlled parts of Europe, Asia, and Africa. In the first century, nearly 54 million people lived in the Roman Empire. Rome, the capital, was one of the largest cities in the world.

By the end of the third century, the empire was in trouble. Powerful invaders threatened its borders. The economy was weak. Many leaders were **corrupt**. This came to be known as the Crisis of the Third Century.

**ROMAN EMPIRE**
THIRD CENTURY A.D.

the Roman Empire in the third century

Emperor Diocletian (dahy-uh-KLEE-shuhn) made an important decision. He split the empire in two. He hoped this would make it easier to rule. Diocletian ruled the Eastern Roman Empire. A different emperor ruled the Western Roman Empire. The Western Roman Empire survived, but not well. The Eastern Roman Empire became strong and powerful. Diocletian had laid the **foundation** for the future.

Emperor Diocletian

The Eastern Roman Empire is known today as the Byzantine (BIZ-uhn-teen) Empire. Under leaders such as Constantine (KON-stuhn-teen) and Justinian I, the empire flourished. The Byzantines preserved the treasures of the ancient world. They created a **unique** culture. Lasting for over a thousand years, the Byzantine Empire shaped the world.

## Too Many Emperors

The Crisis of the Third Century lasted from AD 235 to 285. One of the problems during this time was leadership. During the crisis, there were over 20 different emperors. Most of these emperors ruled for just a few months.

## Rule by Four

Diocletian believed that four rulers would be better than one, so he created a *tetrarchy* (TEH-trahrk-ee), or "rule by four." The Eastern Roman Empire had an Augustus, or senior emperor, and a Caesar (SEE-zer), or junior emperor. The Western Roman Empire had an Augustus and a Caesar, too. Diocletian hoped that four rulers could hold the empire together.

# Emperor Constantine

## Attacking the West

Diocletian was worried about choosing a **successor** to take over as the new emperor. He did not think that sons should take over leadership from their fathers. And at the time, no one considered women to be fit leaders. Diocletian thought emperors should be chosen based on their ability to lead. He decided that when an emperor stepped down, the Caesar would become the new Augustus. Then, a new Caesar would be chosen. But, this plan did not work.

Diocletian's successor died in 306. The successor's son, Constantine, took over as emperor instead of the Augustus. That same year Maxentius (maks-EN-tee-uhs), the son of a former emperor, wanted the power that Constantine claimed. When Maxentius's father died, Maxentius took the role of emperor even though he was not the Caesar.

the Battle of the Milvian Bridge

Constantine sees a vision in the sky at Milvian Bridge.

## In Hoc Signo Vinces

There are many stories about Constantine and his decision to fight under the banner of Christianity. One story states that Constantine saw a vision of a cross in the sky. That night he dreamed that God spoke to him and said, "*In hoc signo vinces.*" This Latin phrase meant "conquer by this sign." Constantine believed God had told him how to win the battle.

## Roman or Byzantine?

People who lived in the Byzantine Empire did not call their empire by that name. They thought of themselves as Romans. It was not until the 18th century that the term *Byzantine* was used to describe the empire.

In 312, Constantine decided to attack Maxentius. He wanted to control the Western Empire. The two armies met in Rome at the Tiber River by the Milvian (MIHL-vee-uhn) Bridge. Even though he was not a Christian, Constantine prayed to the Christian God for victory. He had his men make banners bearing the Christian cross. Constantine's men carried the banners into battle and won. His decision to fight under the banner of Christianity would change the course of world history.

## Attacking the East

The tetrarchy had failed. A system that was designed to reward merit was being changed to promote the son of a former Augustus. After several battles and deaths, it came down to Constantine and Emperor Licinius (lih-SIN-ee-uhs). Emperor Licinius had taken over much of the eastern territories and had become sole emperor. Constantine wanted to defeat Licinius, regain the East, and control the Roman Empire.

## Feudalism

Due to all the fighting, the Roman Empire's economy grew weak. It was hard for people to make enough money to live. Constantine made several changes to get people back to work and help improve the economy. He forced **peasants** to stay on their land and farm. He made sons do the same jobs as their fathers. These changes led to a new social and economic system called *feudalism* (FYOOD-l-iz-uhm).

## The New Rome

Constantine called the city of Constantinople the "New Rome." To Constantine, it was more than just the capital city; it was God's city, the heart of the Christian church. Constantine built many churches, including the Church of the Holy Apostles, the Hagia Irene (AI-yuh AI-reen), and the Hagia Sophia (AI-yuh SOH-fi-uh).

*The Founding of Constantinople*

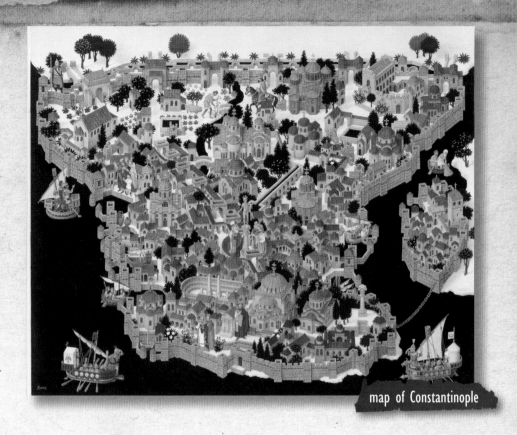

map of Constantinople

In 324, the armies of Licinius and Constantine fought near the ancient Greek city of Byzantium (bih-ZAN-tee-uhm). Constantine's men won the battle. Once again, the Roman Empire was united under one emperor, Constantine the Great.

Since Rome was far away from the main population centers of the East, Constantine wanted to build a new capital closer to the middle of the empire. He thought the old Greek city of Byzantium was the perfect place. The site overlooked the battleground where he had reunited the empire. More importantly, it was situated on the main trade route between the Black Sea and the Mediterranean (med-uh-tuhr-RAY-nee-uhn) Sea. Surrounded on three sides by water, it would be easy to defend. He called the new city Constantinople (kawn-stan-tuh-NO-puhl).

## Constantine and Christianity

During Constantine's time, many people had **pagan** beliefs. They believed in the old Roman gods. When Constantine sent his men to war carrying the Christian cross, everything changed. Constantine created a new relationship between church and state. He used the Christian religion to bring the people together. Constantine joined religious and political powers.

In 313, Constantine issued the **Edict of Milan**. This new law said that Christians would no longer be **persecuted**, or mistreated. Under Constantine, Christianity was accepted. While Constantine did not name Christianity the official religion of the empire, he did make it more acceptable than it had been before.

There were still problems with the church and its teachings. Disagreements about the **divinity** of Jesus threatened to destroy the unity the church had brought to the empire. In 325, Constantine invited all the bishops, or church leaders, of the empire to the city of Nicaea (nai-SEE-uh) to discuss their differences. Constantine convinced the bishops that their differences were not so great. At the meeting in Nicaea, the bishops wrote a document that explained Christian beliefs. That document, the Nicene (NAI-seen) **Creed**, is still used by Christian churches today.

This is the ancient cathedral in Nicaea where the Nicene Creed was written.

## Saint Helena

Constantine's mother, Helena, went on a **pilgrimage**, or religious journey, to Jerusalem (jeh-ROO-suh-luhm). In Jerusalem, Helena built a church at the site of Jesus Christ's tomb called the Church of the Holy Sepulchre (SEP-uhl-ker). For her work helping the poor and preserving the treasures of Christianity, Helena is considered a **saint**.

## The Nicene Creed

Constantine hoped the Nicene Creed, or belief statement, would make the Christian religion easier to understand. He believed more people would adopt Christianity if they understood it. Constantine's creed was "one God, one Lord, one faith, one church, one empire, one emperor."

the meeting in Nicaea

11

Constantine overlooks Constantinople.

# The Byzantine Tradition

### East Versus West

The choices Constantine made set a new course for the Byzantine Empire. He built a new capital over the ruins of an old Greek city. He adopted Christianity. He made important economic changes. Upon his death in 337, rather than choose one leader to take over the empire, Constantine divided it among his three sons.

By the fifth century, the Western Roman Empire was a shadow of its former self. Life there was unruly and violent. However, the eastern half of the empire grew and prospered. The two halves were part of the same empire, but they had become different. Over the years, Roman influence slowly disappeared from the Eastern Empire.

The people of the Eastern Empire thought of themselves as Roman, but their culture was different from that of the Western Empire. Their culture was influenced by Greek traditions more than Roman ones. People of the western lands spoke Latin. In the east, many people spoke Greek. Although both empires were Christian, the people of the east developed unique religious practices.

Constantine converts to Christianity.

## A Diverse People

While the Byzantine tradition was shaped by Roman and Greek culture, it is important to know that a large and diverse group of people made up the empire. Their languages, religious practices, and cultural traditions created what we think of as Byzantine culture.

## All in the Family

Constantine's family had a particular liking for the name Constantine and its various forms. His father was named Constantius. His three sons were Constantine II, Constantius II, and Constans. By the time the Byzantine Empire came to an end in 1453, there had been 12 emperors with the name Constantine, though not all of them were related to Constantine the Great.

## Built to Last

When Constantine first built Constantinople, he carefully planned how to defend it against invaders. The old defensive walls that surrounded Byzantium had mostly fallen apart. Constantine marked out the border of his new city on foot. He used his spear to trace a line showing where he wanted to build the new defensive walls.

By the fifth century, Constantinople had grown so much that it needed more land to support all its people. Emperor Arcadius (ahr-KEYD-ee-uhs) put his engineers to work. He wanted them to design bigger and better walls. It was an enormous project and everyone had to help.

the Theodosian Walls

Theodosius II

The citizens of Constantinople had to pay land taxes to help fund the new walls. They also had to build the walls with their own hands. The walls were made of brick, stone, and lime mortar. Ten gates, or entrances, were built to allow people to enter and leave the city.

The walls were called the Theodosian Walls after Theodosius II (thee-uh-DOH-shee-uhs), who was emperor when the walls were completed. For a thousand years, Constantinople was protected from its enemies because of the strength of its walls.

## Three-Layer Defense

The Theodosian Walls provided three layers of defense. Two thick walls were separated from each other by a walkway. Another walkway connected to a lower wall that formed the inner side of a **moat**.

## Blues Versus Greens

Theodosius II knew his people were competitive. So, he decided to turn the wall-building project into a contest. There would be two teams based on the supporters of Constantinople's two chariot racing teams, the Blues and the Greens. By making it a contest, the people worked faster.

## Justinian the Great

In 527, a new emperor came to the throne who would earn the title "the Great." Justinian I, who was born a poor peasant, became one of the most famous Byzantine emperors in history.

When Justinian became emperor, he named his wife, Theodora, co-emperor. The couple began their reign by reforming the legal system of the empire. They hired legal scholars who wrote a new law code called *Justinian's Code*. The new code influenced European law for centuries.

Justinian was a strict ruler. In 532, the citizens of Constantinople revolted against him in the Nika Rebellion. They destroyed the city of Constantinople. Justinian considered stepping down as emperor until Theodora persuaded him to stay and fight.

Justinian and Theodora

Justinian's Code

the Hagia Sophia

## Nika Rebellion

Justinian made many people unhappy. They did not like the taxes he forced them to pay to improve the empire and support his lavish lifestyle. When they saw Justinian enjoying himself at the chariot races, they became angry. They rushed into the streets shouting, "Nika!" meaning "conquer."

## Hagia Sophia

The Hagia Sophia was one of the earliest Christian churches built in Constantinople. It was built on the orders of Constantine the Great. The original church burned down but was rebuilt by Theodosius II in 405. This church was destroyed during the Nika Rebellion. Justinian rebuilt the church in just six years, making it bigger and more beautiful than it was before.

After the rebellion, Justinian set to work rebuilding the city. He made Constantinople the most beautiful city in Europe. Justinian built new roads, schools, and churches. He strengthened the defensive walls. The most famous of his accomplishments was the rebuilding and expansion of Constantine's church, the Hagia Sophia.

Justinian was not satisfied with rebuilding Constantinople. He wanted to regain much of the empire's lands that had been lost. Justinian's armies re-conquered much of the territories of the old Roman Empire.

## Byzantine Religious Matters

Constantine had brought Christianity to the Byzantine Empire. Later, Emperor Theodosius I had made Christianity the empire's official religion. Because political leaders helped establish the church, there was a close tie between state power and religious power.

Emperor Theodosius I

In Rome, the leader of the church was known as the pope. The **patriarch** of Constantinople was the head of the church in the Eastern Empire. These two men believed they had equal powers. In Constantinople, the emperor had a lot of power over the church. The emperor often made decisions about religious matters.

a Byzantine icon showing the Virgin Mary and Jesus Christ

iconoclasm

## Iconoclasm

The Greek word *Iconoclasm* (ahy-KON-uh-KLAZ-uhm) means "image breaking." Twice in Byzantine history, the leaders of the empire and the church decided to ban the use of icons in worship. These leaders claimed they were following the teachings of **The Ten Commandments** that prohibited worshipping idols.

## Orthodoxy and Catholicism

While both churches share many beliefs, there are also many differences. The Eastern Orthodox Church considers that it is the true church created by Jesus Christ and believes that Jesus Christ is the only leader of the church. The Roman Catholic Church considers the pope to be its leader on earth.

The Byzantines developed different religious traditions from the Roman traditions. One such tradition was using **icons**, or religious images, in worship services. The church in Rome did not like this practice. Emperor Leo III ordered that all icons be destroyed. The Byzantines believed the Western church had no right to get involved in their religious affairs.

By 1054, the two churches had very little in common. Both claimed to be the one true Christian church. Both claimed to practice the true Christian faith. The Christian church split in two. The church in the west became the Roman Catholic Church. The church in the east became the Eastern Orthodox Church.

the Hagia Sophia

Byzantine illuminated manuscript

## Byzantine Architecture

Byzantine **architects** designed and built palaces, churches, and outdoor theaters all around the empire. Byzantine architecture, like Byzantine art, was created to glorify the Christian church. The most prominent features of Byzantine basilicas (buh-SIL-ih-kuhz) are great domes, rounded arches, and large spires.

## Mosaics

Mosaics are images created using small pieces of stone, colored glass, or precious gems. The Byzantines were highly gifted in making mosaics. They made mosaic vases and small portraits, usually with religious themes. Mosaics were often used to decorate the interior spaces of large public buildings.

## Byzantine Art

Christianity influenced Byzantine art. Most art created by the Byzantines was **solemn** (SOL-uhm), or serious. Byzantine artists developed skills in several different art forms. They painted and made **mosaics** (moh-ZEY-iks). Some artists carved ivory and others made **illuminations**. These were special texts illustrated with artworks made from paints that contained silver or gold. The illustrations seemed to glow with a heavenly light.

Whatever the art form, the theme was most often religious. Since the church and state were so closely tied, art works portraying emperors often showed them as holy figures. They regularly wore halos or were made to look divine, or godly.

Most figures in Byzantine art are flat and one-dimensional. The expressions on the faces of figures in paintings and mosaics seem emotionless or sad. Artists did not attempt to make figures seem lifelike or happy. During the eighth and ninth centuries, it was forbidden to paint the likenesses of people. This was mainly due to the beliefs of Emperor Leo III. He believed that painting people was a form of **idolatry** (ahy-DOL-uh-tree), or idol worship. Idolatry was against church teachings.

mosaics in the Hagia Sophia

# Under Attack

## Surrounded by Enemies

The problem with building a powerful empire and a grand city is that neighboring empires become **envious**, or jealous. This was true for the Byzantine Empire. Enemies surrounded it. By the seventh century, a new threat appeared in the east. Arab armies were on the move. Egypt and North Africa fell quickly to them. Jerusalem fell to the Arab armies, too. The only city that did not fall to the attackers was Constantinople. The walled city was protected for the time being.

This map shows the areas controlled by the Byzantine Empire and the Seljuk Turks.

Greek fire

## Greek Fire

The Byzantines developed a secret weapon that gave them an important advantage in naval warfare. This weapon was known as "Greek fire." The Byzantines would shoot a flaming substance onto their enemies' ships. It was a quick burning liquid that was difficult to put out. Not even water could put out its flames.

## The Battle of Manzikert

The Seljuk Turks, a nomadic tribe from Central Asia, were able to defeat the Byzantines at Manzikert. This battle is thought to have opened the door for other invaders from the east, who eventually brought the Byzantine Empire to an end.

Inside the empire, there were many problems. While there were several emperors who worked in the best interest of the empire, there were many who only cared about improving their own lives. The poor were unfairly taxed. The rich estate holders took over more and more land. Small farmers ended up as **serfs**, or enslaved laborers, on lands they formerly owned. By the tenth century, the empire was crumbling from within.

In 1064, another enemy threatened the Byzantine Empire. The Seljuk (SEL-jook) Turks attacked Armenia (ahr-MEE-nee-uh). Armenia was a frontier region of the empire. In 1071, the Byzantine army fought against the Seljuk army at Manzikert (MAN-zih-kurt). The Byzantines were defeated. This battle signaled the beginning of the end for the Byzantine Empire.

Christians win control of Jerusalem.

## The Fourth Crusade

In 1095, Pope Urban II of the Roman Catholic Church called on Christians to take back Jerusalem in a holy war against the Turks. The Crusades, or "wars of the cross," were a series of wars between Christians and Muslims. Both sides wanted to control the holy city of Jerusalem. During the First Crusade, Christians won control of Jerusalem. By 1174, a strong **Kurdish** general, Saladin (SAL-uh-dihn), put together a powerful fighting force and regained control of Jerusalem for the Turks.

After Saladin died, European leaders decided the time was right to begin another crusade. They made a new plan to attack from the south using ships, instead of from the north by land.

The crusaders went to the seaport city of Venice to buy ships and get more men to join the fight. They did not have enough money to buy all the ships they needed. A young prince named Alexius (uh-LEK-see-uhs) saw a great opportunity. With the help of a German king, Alexius convinced the crusaders to help him fight for control of Constantinople. If they helped him, he promised to pay for the crusade.

In 1204, the crusaders stormed Constantinople from the sea. They burned the city, destroyed churches and houses, and looted all of the gold and jewels they could find.

## Sea Walls

The sea walls surrounding Constantinople had protected the city since the fourth century. During the Fourth Crusade, the attacking crusader armies used ladders and crossbeams to climb over the walls. This time the walls could not save the city from its enemies.

## Stolen Statues

The crusaders who attacked Constantinople destroyed many great works of ancient literature, art, and religion. Many statues were taken from Constantinople to Venice. One famous statue of four bronze horses known as the Triumphal Quadriga (trahy-UHM-fuhl kwa-DREE-guh) can be seen today atop Saint Mark's Basilica in Venice. The Western world knows this statue as the Horses of Saint Mark's.

the Horses of Saint Mark's

## Ottoman Invaders

Although they had feared Turkish invaders from the east, it was European crusaders that brought down the Byzantine Empire. After the Fourth Crusade, the Byzantine Empire went into a long decline. Civil wars and economic problems weakened the empire. Still, the Byzantines managed to struggle along.

By 1453, all that remained of the Byzantine Empire was the city of Constantinople. At one time it had been the most magnificent city in the world. Now Constantinople was crumbling. The people of the city were poor. The beautiful palaces and churches were falling apart. But because of its location between the East and the West, Constantinople was an important possession. New invaders set their sights on the city.

Mehmet II

A **nomadic** tribe from Central Asia, the Ottoman Turks, appeared in the east. They took advantage of the weakened conditions of Constantinople and attacked. For six weeks, the Ottomans, led by Mehmet II (MEH-met), pounded the city walls with cannon fire. Finally, they broke through. Mehmet paraded through the gate with his conquering army. The Byzantine Empire was no more.

## Islam

When the Ottoman Turks conquered the Byzantine Empire they brought their own religion, Islam, with them. The Ottomans did not require people to convert to Islam, but many did. The Ottomans tolerated Christianity, but forced the Christians to pay higher taxes.

## The Ottoman Empire

The Ottoman Turks built a strong and powerful empire. From the late thirteenth century until 1923, the Ottomans ruled the Anatolian (an-uh-TOH-lee-uhn) peninsula and more. Over time, the Ottomans suffered from many of the same problems as the Byzantines. Jealous neighbors, fights over succession, and economic problems weakened them. The Ottoman Empire eventually collapsed and modern-day Turkey was born.

The Ottoman Turks invade Constantinople.

# Byzantines Shape the World

Historians sometimes disagree about the nature of the Byzantine Empire. They argue about whether it was simply an extension of the Roman Empire or a unique empire of its own. It is clear that the empire preserved treasures and traditions of the past, but it also created a unique culture of its own. The Byzantines embraced Christianity, yet gave birth to a new religious tradition, Eastern Orthodoxy.

The Byzantines had a great influence on cultural and religious developments in Russia. Russian Prince Vladimir I (VLAD-uh-meer) adopted Orthodox Christianity from the Byzantines. Later, Orthodox Christianity became the state religion of the Russian Empire.

Constantinople was, for a time, one of the most successful and beautiful cities in the world. It was a **crossroads** between the East and West. It was a place where people traded goods and ideas. The treasures of the ancient world were preserved in Constantinople.

When Constantinople began to decline, many people fled to Western Europe. They took with them the great literary and artistic treasures of the past. These works appeared later in Italy. They helped start a rebirth, or new beginning, of culture and learning. This would later be known as the **Renaissance**.

## Eastern Orthodoxy in Russia

The Byzantines had great influence over cultural, artistic, economic, and social developments in Russia. The most significant influence was in the area of religion. According to legend, Prince Vladimir I sent ambassadors out to study the religions of his neighboring states. The ambassadors who returned from Constantinople described the beauty and majesty of the city by saying, "we no longer knew if we were in heaven or on earth." Vladimir understood that a good relationship with the Byzantines would be politically and economically beneficial.

the christening of Prince Vladimir

# Glossary

**architects**—people who design buildings

**corrupt**—guilty of dishonest practices

**creed**—a statement of belief

**crossroads**—a main center of activity

**divinity**—a divine being

**Edict of Milan**—a statement made by rulers that said Christians could practice their religion without fear of persecution

**envious**—to be jealous of someone's success

**feudalism**—the social and economic system of medieval Europe

**foundation**—the support or base on which something else is built

**iconoclasm**—a Greek word that means "image breaking"

**icons**—images of someone or something sacred

**idolatry**—the religious worship of an image of a god

**illuminations**—books that contain artistic images, often made from paints containing silver or gold

**Kurdish**—a member of a nomadic people who live in a region near the Middle East

**moat**—a deep trench, usually filled with water, surrounding a castle, used as a protective barrier

**mosaics**—pictures or decorations made of small pieces of glass or stone

**nomadic**—a group of people who have no permanent home and moves from place to place

**pagan**—a person who worships many gods or does not worship any god

**patriarch**—the father-like figure considered to be the leader of a group

**peasants**—members of the agricultural class

**persecuted**—treated harshly because of one's own beliefs

**pilgrimage**—a journey to a holy place to show devotion

**Renaissance**—a period of time in which European culture experienced a revival of art, science, and literature

**saint**—a title given to someone of great holiness by the Christian church

**serfs**—peasants or people who worked the land in a feudal system

**solemn**—serious

**successor**—a person that follows another into political office

**superpowers**—extremely powerful nations

**Ten Commandments, The**—according to Judeo-Christian tradition, the ten important laws given by God to Moses

**unique**—unlike anything or anyone; original

# Index

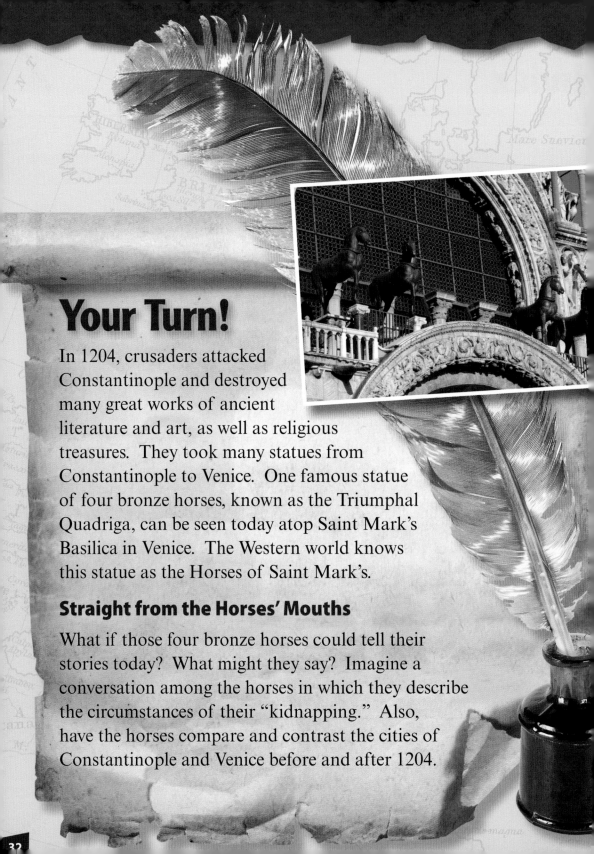

# Your Turn!

In 1204, crusaders attacked Constantinople and destroyed many great works of ancient literature and art, as well as religious treasures. They took many statues from Constantinople to Venice. One famous statue of four bronze horses, known as the Triumphal Quadriga, can be seen today atop Saint Mark's Basilica in Venice. The Western world knows this statue as the Horses of Saint Mark's.

## Straight from the Horses' Mouths

What if those four bronze horses could tell their stories today? What might they say? Imagine a conversation among the horses in which they describe the circumstances of their "kidnapping." Also, have the horses compare and contrast the cities of Constantinople and Venice before and after 1204.